The Wonder of Stillness

Meditation for Children

A Practical Guide for Parents and Teachers

by Michelle Sorrell

Illustrations by Caroline Kilduff

Published by Stillness Publishing

Illustrations by Caroline Kilduff

Setting by Loulita Gill Design

Printed through SS Media Ltd
Rickmansworth Hertfordshire

ISBN: 978-1-9160995-0-0

A catalogue record of this book is available from the British Library.

Dedication

Dedicated to my brother Sacha,
a man of purpose, passion and kindness, who encouraged
and inspired me to write this book.

Contents

Introduction **7**
What is Meditation? **11**
Mindfulness **15**
Practical Guidance **17**
Infants **23**
Meditations **25**

Calming Meditations **27**
The Breath of Life 29
Tranquil Pond 33
Sunset 37
Gentle Waves 41
The Tree 45
Uplifting Meditations **49**
Birdsong 51
Springtime 55
Sailing 59
Puppy Life 63
Fun in the Snow 67

Creativity **71**
Pebble on a beach 73
Autumn Leaves 77
Frosty Day 81
Cloud Gazing 85
Cosmic Journey 89

Confidence Meditations **93**
The Sun 95
Secret Smile 99
Animal Adventure 103
Your Loving Higher Self 107
The Mountain 111
The Perfect Zonev 115

Self Healing **119**
The Candle 121
Magical Waters 125
Shower of Light 129
The Rainbow 133
The Healing Heart Centre 137

Resources and References **141**
The Seven Chakras 141
Music for meditation 142
Sprays 143
References 144
Further Reading 145

Final Words **147**

Introduction

My main purpose in writing this book is to help children discover the magic of stillness and find a place of inner peace and tranquillity. Stillness is a state of being that allows us to connect to our deepest essence. For children, who tend to be active, meditation provides the opportunity to experience quiet time and a space to be still and reflect. Meditation shows children how to learn to journey inside and discover a world that can bring them peace and joy.

The exercises in this book instruct children how to breathe fully (see Meditation 'Breath of Life'). They also include techniques for reducing stress, building confidence, increasing creativity, self-healing and dealing with life's many challenges. Once children have learned the basics of meditation they have a tool that they can continue to use during their teenage and adult years to help them step away from the busyness and pressures of everyday life, including technology and social media.

This is a practical guide for school teachers, yoga teachers, parents, carers, family and friends and is based on my own experience of teaching meditation to children. I have included a section titled 'Practical Guidance' and Notes at the beginning of each meditation to provide tips and ideas for creating a positive environment for meditation and guiding children through the exercises. The meditations are aimed at children aged 3 to 11 years. For children under 3 years of age please refer to the section on 'Infants'.

I highly recommend that a selection of the meditations are practiced before reading them out to children in order to experience and understand the benefits that meditation may offer. The scripts in this book can be used as a stepping-stone to develop your own visualisations, meditations and stories to inspire children.

Our educational system has focused on developing the intellect of children at the cost of developing their intuition, creativity and imagination. An important aim of this book is to help redress the balance of our education system from its emphasis on '*left brain*' activities such as logic, analytical thought, science, maths and reasoning to '*right brain*' activities such as insight, intuition, creativity, arts appreciation and imagination. A more equal balance between both types of activity is needed.

Meditation can help to develop intuition, insight and imagination. (See section 'What is Meditation?')

Many of the meditations include imagery focused in the natural world with the aim of inspiring interest in and bringing children closer to nature. The movement towards outdoors (or forest) schooling where children learn outside in forests and woodlands has many positive benefits including improving wellbeing, developing imagination and building confidence.[1]

When working with children it is important to acknowledge the different stages of children's development. According to Alice Bailey "*in teaching children up to fourteen years of age, it is necessary to bear in mind that they are emotionally focused. They need to feel, and rightly to feel beauty, strength and wisdom.*"[2] There are schools and programmes such as the Steiner Waldorf educational system that recognise the importance of working in harmony with the different phases of children's development.[3]

In their emotionally focused state, children may be more in touch with the magical qualities of their inner and outer world. Their imagination is boundless and their potential for creativity has no limits. Meditation gives them space to explore their feelings and senses and expand their imagination before they embark on their teenage years. It provides children with the opportunity to discover their uniqueness and their own special gifts to work on and develop as they grow into adults.

Incorporating daily meditation practice into home and school routines helps to support the emotional, mental and spiritual development of children. Now is the time to give children back their childhood and guide them to develop into conscious, clear thinking and healthy individuals with loving hearts and well balanced minds.

What is Meditation?

Meditation has been described as "*deep and continuous thought that allows us to travel inward.... The act of meditation can cause our brain waves to slow down to such a degree that we use more of our mind. This action, once achieved, allows us to reflect on the inner aspects of mind.*"[4]

There are five stages of meditation that consist of Concentration, Meditation, Contemplation, Illumination, and Inspiration.[5] This book focuses on the first two stages of Concentration and Meditation.

Concentration

Concentration is the practice of gaining control of the mind. It is the gathering together of wandering thoughts and ideas and holding the mind firmly, focusing on the object of immediate attention. One effective way to learn to concentrate is to replace unwanted thoughts with new thoughts and a fresh focus of attention.

Meditation

Meditation is the prolonged holding of attention in a certain area. "*The mind remains focused and is continually active throughout the meditation period.*"[6] During meditation, we notice any thoughts that arise in our minds and let them go rather than trying to make the mind blank.

In my experience, both Concentration and Meditation can be developed using simple breathing and visualisation techniques. By focusing on the action of breathing in and out, all the attention is brought to the rhythm of the breath and to the present moment. The guided visualisation exercises help to sustain and prolong mind control by bringing in new pictures and ideas rather than letting the mind wander.

Imagination

Imagination is an important tool for developing creativity as it "*links with sensation, feeling, thinking and also intuition*".[7] Using imagery is the best way to train creative imagination. Exercises to train the imagination should be constructive or positive and the length of time for the exercise should be decided in advance. Here is an exercise based upon an example provided by MJ Eastcott to train the imagination:[8]

The Garden

Imagine an area of grass surrounded by a fence
Take a few minutes to build up the picture of the grass and the fence
Then include more detail, adding colourful flowers,
plants and trees and make the garden complete

Now step into garden
Imagine the warmth and light of the sun shining down on you
and the sounds and scents in the air

Enjoy these sensations for a minute, always remaining the observer
Then after 2 minutes deliberately withdraw and dismiss the picture

Imagination can be used constructively to help with facing difficult situations. By seeing ourselves go through a situation successfully, we can learn to eliminate fear and anxious anticipation. Negative emotions can then be replaced with a positive attitude.[9] (See Meditation 'The Perfect Zone').

There are many benefits to the regular practice of meditation including reduction of stress, increased creativity and imagination, better focus and sleep and improved mind health. Studies have shown benefits for patients engaging in a mindfulness meditation programme in areas such as depression, chronic pain, and anxiety.[10]

Mindfulness

Mindfulness is the bringing of attention to the present moment without any judgment. The focus on breathing throughout the meditations helps children to experience mindfulness. This practice can be extended to many other activities for example:

Mindful Walking

Ideally this exercise should be practiced outside. Remove shoes (and socks if the ground/grass is suitable for barefoot walking) and feel the ground underneath your feet. Standing up straight take a deep breath in and out. Then bring the focus to the physical movement of taking a step. Carefully lift up one foot, balancing on the other leg and slowly transfer your body weight to place the foot firmly on the ground. Repeat with the other foot and continue the slow walking, paying attention to the sensation of the ground underneath and every single physical movement. Try walking in time with the breath using an in breath to lift a foot and out breath when placing the foot on the ground.

Allow the breath to last as long as possible. Practice the exercise for at least 5 minutes.

Mindful eating

Pick up a piece of food and look carefully at its shape and colour. Notice whether it is warm or cold in your hand. Think about where the food came from. It may be a piece of fruit picked from a tree or a piece of bread made from wheat. Smell the piece of food carefully and then place it on your tongue. Feel its texture for a few moments. Leave the food for as long as possible on the tongue and let it dissolve. Savour the taste of the food as long as possible until the food has disappeared.

These exercises may be adapted to practice with children. Raisins are very popular for mindful eating exercises.

Practical Guidance

The majority of the guidance applies both to parents at home and teachers in a classroom, gymnasium, studio or other location. The term "classroom" is used for convenience. Any differences are described where appropriate below.

Setting up the room

At home, set aside a special place for meditation such as the corner of a room or bedroom. Let your child decorate the space with candles, cushions, a rug and any other items they choose. Arrange the area so you can sit opposite your child or in small circle if you are practising the meditation with a few children.

In the classroom, arrange chairs (including your own) in a circle or sit the children on yoga mats or cushions in a circle on the floor. A small table or tray can be placed in the centre of the circle for a candle, flowers or to display objects that relate to the meditation exercise.

Posture

It is important to have a straight spine during meditation to align the energy centres in the body. (See 'The Seven Chakras' in the Resources section). You can encourage children to sit up straight by asking them to imagine an invisible string pulling them up from the top of their heads to ceiling or sky above. Sitting on the edge of a cushion can also help to support a straight back. If additional encouragement is needed, then demonstrate rolling your shoulders backwards and forwards before sitting up straighter. Gentle twists and stretches may also help.

Use of Music

Music can enhance the atmosphere and help children enter into a relaxed and calm state. The volume of the music should be at a suitable level to allow you to be heard clearly. Recommendations for DVDs and websites are included in the Resources section.

Materials

Plan ahead and have drawing or painting materials available such as pencils, crayons, felt tip pens and paints (including silver and gold colours if possible) for use after the meditation. Children are particularly creative after a meditation and you may be surprised by the results. It is also helpful to share images of the scenes and places described during meditations and items related to the exercises such as pebbles, flowers and leaves.

Selecting the Meditation Exercise

The exercises are divided into five categories:

1. Calming
2. Uplifting
3. Creativity
4. Confidence
5. Self-Healing

The meditations in the Calming section are intended to help children pause and be still. The other four categories are more energetic. You may wish to choose an exercise that relates to the season or time of year. Alternatively, select a few exercises from each of the categories and assess the state of the child or children before deciding the exercise that you believe will be most helpful. For example, if a child is stressed or has very high energy then choose a calming meditation. If a group of children are bored or their energy is low then select an uplifting exercise. You may find it beneficial to choose a creative meditation before an art class or creative writing class.

Age appropriate meditations

The shorter meditations are more appropriate for the younger children (aged 3 to 6 years) and the longer meditations involving more complex visualisation exercises are more suitable for older children (aged 7 to 11 years). You can adapt the meditations to suit the age of the children, for example by adding in your own imagery or omitting a paragraph. In addition, include longer pauses for older children to provide a longer period for reflection.

Preparation before reading out the Meditation

Before starting to read out the meditation, take a few moments to breathe deeply and ensure you are calm and focused. A few gentle coughs and a sip of water may help to clear your throat. Here is an exercise to assist:

Close your eyes and take three deep breaths
breathing in through your nose and out through your mouth

See yourself as calm and peaceful
as you read out the meditation to the children
who are focused on your every word

See the children as calm and peaceful at the end of the meditation
Take another 3 deep breaths
Open your eyes when you are ready

Reading out the Meditation

Read out the chosen meditation exercise as slowly as possible and pause for at least three seconds between each line of the exercise. Allow yourself to go with the flow of the words and establish a rhythm that suits you. You will need to adjust your voice to suit the size of the room and the number of children. Parents may find it effective to use a gentle voice with one or a small number of children. Teachers may need to use more intonation and project their voices to keep a classroom engaged. It is worthwhile practicing the chosen meditation a few times before reading it out.

Affirmations

An affirmation is a positive statement that can be used to enhance confidence and self-belief, for example "I am Confident and Brave", "I am a Being of Light" and "I am Loved and Loving". Affirmations are included in some of the meditations in this book. Do include additional affirmations that are appropriate to the meditation exercise.

Chanting

Sounding out words such as 'OM' (pronounced AUM) three times at the end of a meditation practice creates a vibrational tone that has an uplifting effect. You can include chants at the beginning or end of each practice according to your cultural or social environment, for example "Om, Om Shalom".

Regularity of practice

Daily practice, first thing in the morning is ideal time for meditation. This may be achievable at home, but in a school environment it may be more difficult. Encourage the children to practice a simple exercise such as 'The Breath of Life' at home each morning to help them establish a routine.

Infants

It is quite challenging for children under the age of three years to sit still and meditate for any period of time. Instead, you can help infants to relax by encouraging them to lie down on a mat or carpet on the floor and do the relaxation exercise below. This exercise is also helpful before bedtime.

Relaxation Exercise

Ask the children to lie down in a comfortable position with their arms by their sides, palms facing up. Before you start, demonstrate belly breathing by placing your hands on your tummy, allowing your tummy to rise as you breathe in and flatten as you breathe out.

Close your eyes and put your hands on your belly
As you breathe in your belly rises up
As you breathe out make a loud sigh
and feel your tummy becoming flat

Think about your toes and wiggle them about
As you breathe in scrunch up your toes
hold them tight and release them as you breathe out

Think about your feet, breathe in and point your feet
and as you breath out relax your feet
Now think about your legs
as you breathe in squeeze your legs tightly
and as you breathe out
allow them to become soft like jelly

Next think about your fingers and wiggle them about
As you breathe in make a tight fist with your hands
as you breathe out relax your fingers and hands
letting them become soft

Breathe in and bring your shoulders right up to your ears
as you breathe out let your shoulders fall down and relax

Make a funny face as you breathe in,
as you breathe out let your face soften
and allow your eyes, ears, mouth and head to relax

Now take a deep breath in and squeeze every muscle of your body,
and breathe out slowly with a sign
As you do this, let every muscle become soft
until your whole body feels relaxed

Young children may enjoy having lavender scented bean bags over their eyes during this exercise. They also love sprays containing sweet smelling essential oils. You can spray the area above the children before commencing the relaxation exercise. The sprays are easy to make and a recipe is provided in the Resources section.

Meditations

Calming / Uplifting / Creativity
Confidence / Self-Healing

Calming Meditations

- The Breath of Life
- Tranquil Pond
- Sunset
- Gentle Waves
- The Tree

The Breath of Life

Notes

Breathing is essential to life. It is one of the most effective ways to calm down our nervous system and reduce stressful patterns. We can use breathing to control our thoughts, reactions, emotions and behaviours.

Here is a simple exercise to reduce panic and calm down especially before a test, exam or other stressful situation. There are three stages of breathing in this exercise: inhalation, retention and exhalation. If this exercise is practised regularly, the children will be able to inhale, hold the breath and exhale for longer periods of time.

Meditation

Close your eyes
Place your hands gently on the sides of your ribs
Breathe in through your nose for 2 counts
feel your lungs expanding
Hold your breath for 2 counts
then breathe out through your mouth for 4 counts

And again, breathe in through your nose for 2 counts
Hold for 2 counts
and breathe out through your mouth for 4 counts

Notice how your body feels now

Let's try breathing in for 3 counts
Hold your breath for 3 counts
And breathe out for 6 counts

This time breathe in positive, happy energy
As you hold your breath
notice the quiet and stillness around you

As you breathe out,
let go of any feelings or thoughts
that may make you worried or unhappy
Let's do this again

Now as you breathe in
see a stream of white light
flowing down over your body
As you hold your breath
spread the light through your body

As you breathe out
send rays of light out from your body
to fill the whole room and then the whole building,
you can send the rays to fill the whole city, the country
even the whole world
you can go even further into space
Spread your light as far as you wish….

Return to normal breathing
Notice any further changes to your body
or your feelings
Open your eyes when you are ready

Tranquil Pond

Notes

This exercise helps children to calm down and experience stillness, peace and tranquillity. Visualising still water can help to calm down emotions and reduce anxiety and stress levels.

Meditation

Sitting comfortably, gently close your eyes
Take a deep breath in through your nose
and slowly breathe out through your mouth
And again breathe in and breathe out
And one more breath in and out

Return to normal breathing
Breathing in and out through your nose

In your mind
See yourself entering into a green forest
on a warm summer's day
See yourself walking under large trees
with the sun shining down on you through the leaves

You follow a path up a gentle hill
Until you reach a pond
at the top of the hill

The water is greeny/blue and still
Trees surround the pond
And you can see a perfect reflection of the trees in the water

Notice a bird standing on an island
in the centre of the pond
The bird is as still as a statue
Pause by the pond
and become as still as the bird

Then sit down on a log near to the pond
Look into the water
So you can see your own reflection

You are as still as the water
There is no movement or sound
apart from your breathing

Listen to your breathing
For a few moments
Let yourself become calm and peaceful
Connect to the stillness inside of you

Take three more deep breaths
In through your nose and out through your mouth
When you are ready open your eyes

Sunset

Notes

This is a calming exercise for any time of the year. It also assists with visualisation and creative imagination. Share a photo of a sunset over the sea before starting the meditation. Let the child or children explore and discuss the range of colours and share their experiences of seeing sunsets.

Children may be inspired to draw a sunset after the exercise so have a rich palette of colours available including, purple, pink, red, orange and yellow and suitable paper and other drawing materials.

Meditation

Close your eyes
Take a deep breath in through your nose
and slowly breathe out through your mouth
Return to normal breathing
Breathing in and out through your nose

Picture in your mind the sun setting over the sea
See yourself sitting on a beach watching a sunset
See the colours in the sky
the pinks, reds, oranges and purple
And the sun itself,
a golden ball slowly moving down towards the sea

Notice the reflection of the sky in the water
The colours rippling in the waves
as they draw towards the shore

Let's take three deep breaths together
in time with the rhythm of the waves
moving forwards and back again

Breath in and breathe out
And again breathe in and out
And once again breathe in and out

Feel the peace and calmness around you

Look up at the sunset once again
The colours are filling the sky
The sun drops close to the sea
And starts to disappear
Leaving traces of pink and orange behind

Soon it will be dark and night-time will arrive
Tomorrow the sun will rise again
And so the cycle continues
Day to night and night to day

Take another deep breath in and out
and open your eyes

Gentle Waves

Notes

This is a calming meditation. The waves in this exercise are gentle and purifying, washing away any stress or anxieties. Find a recording of waves lapping onto the shore and play it softly as background music during the meditation.

Meditation

Take three deep breaths,
Breathe in through your nose and out through your mouth
Return to normal breathing
Breathing in and out through your nose

See yourself sitting under a palm tree
on a tropical beach on a hot, sunny day

Hear the sound of the waves
The sea is turquoise
The sky is blue
and there is a gentle breeze in the air

Walk towards the sea
Your feet sinking into the warm, white sand
and step into the water

It is refreshing and cool
Small waves cover your ankles
Step over the next wave
until the water reaches your knees

The ripples of white foaming water
now cover your legs

Keep walking into the sea until the waves
Cover your hips and tummy
As you walk further into the sea
the water becomes calm and peaceful

Lie on your back
And let yourself float
feeling the gentle movement of the water
under your body

The sun shines over you
Smell the saltiness of the sea
Let yourself feel the sensation of peace and quiet

The waves gently carry you back
to the shore

Take three deep breaths
In through your nose and out through your mouth
And open your eyes when you are ready

The Tree

Notes

Trees represent strength, stability and protection. With roots reaching deep down into the earth, trees are regarded as having a 'grounding' effect, making one feel centred and balanced. Their trunks and branches extend up towards the sky and their leaves provide shade and cover from the elements. This meditation is intended to provide support and help children feel calm and peaceful.

Meditation

Sitting comfortably
Gently close your eyes
Bring your attention to your breathing
Slowly breathe in through your nose
And breathe out through your mouth with a sigh

Return to normal breathing in and out through your nose

See yourself walking in a park
on a warm, summer's day

See colourful flowers and plants all around
Passing by a pond
notice if any ducks are paddling in the water

Continue walking until you see a large tree ahead
It is the largest tree in the park
with a wide trunk extending up to the sky
and long, thick branches
covered with shiny green leaves

Walk right up to the tree
And place your hands gently on its trunk
Notice whether the bark is rough or smooth
Look closely as its colour

With your hands on the trunk
Bring your attention to your breathing
Allow yourself to become calm and still like the tree

Now sit down at the base of the tree
With your back resting against the trunk
The tree is supporting you
And providing you with cover and protection

Imagine that you are tree
With roots pushing down into the ground
And your body and head extending up to the sky
You feel balanced and stable

Take another deep breath in through your nose
And slowly breathe out through your mouth

Return back to the room
and when you are ready open your eyes
feeling calm and refreshed

Uplifting Meditations

- Birdsong
- Springtime
- Sailing
- Puppy Life
- Fun in the Snow

Birdsong

Notes

Birdsong has high, chirpy tones that are uplifting and energising. This meditation vitalises children and helps to enhance their sense of listening. This exercise introduces children to the connection between colour, light and vibration.

There are a number of questions raised during the meditation. Before starting, ask the children to answer the questions in their heads and encourage them to talk about their senses and feelings after the exercise.

It is helpful to play a recording of birdsong before the exercise. Continue to play the recording during the meditation at a level the children can hear clearly during the exercise. Children can be encouraged to do this practice when they wake up in the morning and tune in the birdsong outside their window.

Meditation

Close your eyes
Take a deep breath in through your nose
and breathe out through your mouth
Return to normal breathing
breathing in and out through your nose

Bring your attention to your ears
Tune into your own sense of hearing
What can you hear in this room right now?

Listen carefully to the birdsong
Listen to each and every note being sung

Picture in your mind birds singing
Sitting on a branch high up on a tree
under a blue sky with the sun shining brightly

How many birds can you hear singing?
Is it only one bird or many more?

Listen out for different songs, rhythms and sounds
that the birds are making
Notice how many different tunes you can hear

How does the birdsong make you feel?
Does it make you think of any colours?
You can describe your feelings and the colours later on

Take a deep breath in through your nose
Breathing in the sounds to every cell in your body
and breathing out any positive feelings you have inside
like happiness and joy

And again, breathing in the sounds of the birdsong
And as you breathe out, spread out happiness and joy
or any other positive feelings you have

Lets do this again, breathing in the birdsong
and breathing out

When you are ready open your eyes

Springtime

Notes

This is an uplifting meditation for springtime or any time of the year, particularly if your child or children need to uplifted or inspired. Gather some blossoms and spring flowers such as daffodils and tulips to decorate the room. Alternatively, ask children to collect blossoms or flowers and lay them out in the centre of the meditation area. Ask the children to smell the blossoms or flowers before starting the exercise. It is helpful to explain that this exercise takes place in spring and ensure younger children are aware of the rest of the seasons in the year.

Meditation

Close your eyes
Bring your attention to your breathing
Notice the rhythm of your breath
as you breathe in and out through your nose

Breathing has a natural rhythm
like the waves in the sea
the change of day into night
and the change of seasons
from spring to summer,
to autumn and then winter
and back to spring again

Life is full of rhythm and change

See yourself taking a walk in a park
on a warm day in spring

Take a deep breath in through your nose
and notice the smell of the blossoms
and spring flowers around you

The sun is shining in the blue sky
There are new buds on branches
Young flowers and plants are growing
Insects are out flying over flowers
Birds are singing in the trees

There is new life and joy all around you

Sit down in the soft, green grass
Breathing in the sounds, scents and sights
of Springtime

Take a deep breath in and out
Open your eyes when you are ready

Sailing

Notes

This is an uplifting and energising meditation. Water is often depicted as representing emotions and so navigating the waves is symbolic of how a child can learn to deal with their emotions.

Find a photo of a sailing boat and point out the main areas of the boat e.g. the mast, the sails and the wheel before starting the meditation.

Meditation

Close your eyes
and listen to the sound of your breathing
The gentle in-breath and out-breath

Picture a sailing boat in your mind
See the tall mast
and two large white sails
flapping in the wind

See yourself in a harbour on a fresh and windy day
Many sailing boats are lined up next to each other
Large and small, narrow and wide
White, blue, green and brown

Walk along until you reach the boat
that you are going to sail
You can choose the name for the boat
Just think of a name in your head
and see it appear on the side of the boat

Climb up onto the boat
holding onto a rope
As you climb up
the captain greets you

Help untie the ropes at the front and back of the boat
The captain is ready to leave the harbour
And takes the boat out into the open sea
Feel the waves bobbing up and down under the boat
A gust of wind blows through your hair
And it is time to release the sails

With a whoosh.... the sails are untied
and filled with air
taking the boat faster and faster over the waves

The boat leans right over to the left
as it turns direction and then levels off
Then the boat leans to the right
And back up straight again

The winds settle down
There is just a gentle breeze in the air
The sun comes out and shines over the water
Glistening, silvery water surrounds you

Feel the waves under the boat
and the rhythm of the up and down, up and down
Take three deep breaths in through your nose
and out through your mouth

Return to gentle breathing
in time with the rhythm of the waves

The captain calls you over
And lets you take the wheel
You steer the large wheel
over the gentle waves

Ahead is an island
You steer the boat gently towards it
The sails are folded up
Ropes are thrown overboard
and tied up to the landing bay

You have reached your destination
over the waves, both fierce and strong
Gentle and calm
Across the sea
In your sailing boat

Puppy Life

Notes

This exercise is stimulating and uplifting. At home, share photos or pictures of dogs or puppies before the exercise. At school, encourage children to bring in photos of their pets. This is likely to cause excitement so be prepared to do some breathing exercises to settle the children before you start.

Remind the children to answer any questions in their heads during the meditation and encourage them to share their stories after the exercise.

Meditation

Close your eyes
Notice your gentle breathing
in and out through your nose

Picture a puppy in your mind
Think about its colour
It may be black, brown, white or ginger

The puppy may have long or short, curly or straight hair
The puppy may be large or small,
playful or shy

Think about a name for the puppy

Now imagine that you are that puppy
running across a green field
on a warm summer's day

See a bird and chase it
There are amazing smells in the air
in the grass and from the flowers and trees

A child throws a ball up high in the sky
You jump up to try to catch it in your mouth
and chase it as it lands and rolls away

A fluffy black dog runs past you,
chase the dog and you play together for a while
Life is so much fun and full of adventure

Birds are flying above
Butterflies and bees swarm over flowers
There is so much activity around you!

Lie back in the soft grass
and take a rest looking up
at the birds flying above

It is time to return to your own body as a human
Remember the joy of being a puppy
You can go back to that place anytime you wish.

Take a deep breath in through your nose
and breathe out through your mouth
Open your eyes when you are ready

Fun in the Snow

Notes

Activities in the snow such as throwing snowballs, building snowmen and sledging are joyful and uplifting. This meditation is aimed at reviving children during the long winter months. It can also be used to promote creativity and imagination.

Share some pictures of snowflakes, a snowy landscape or any snow activity to remind children of the purity and beauty of a snowy environment. Have suitable drawing materials available for example, white, yellow and grey chalk or pencils and dark paper for the children to use afterwards.

Meditation

Close your eyes
Take a deep breath in through your nose
And breathe out through your mouth

Picture in your mind a snowy day
Your home, garden, the street and pavements
are covered with a thick layer of white snow

Warmly dressed, with a coat, hat, gloves and scarf
see yourself opening a door and walking outside
into a magical white world

Step into the soft, fluffy snow
Look behind to see your footprints
As you step into the deep, soft snow

The sky is white
The houses, cars, roads and trees
are covered with a white blanket
The brightness of the snow is all around you

Snowflakes start to gently fall from the sky
Catch one in your hand
Look at its colour, shape and patterns before it melts
Notice how delicate it is

Collect the snow and make a snowball
It is cold and firm
Make as many snowballs as you wish
Now you can build a snowman or make a giant snowball

Spend a few minutes creating something
out of the snow
It may be any shape you wish

Remember the details of what you have made
So you can draw it later

When you have finished,
take a deep breath in through your nose
and breathe out through your mouth with a sigh
And find yourself back in this room

Open your eyes when you are ready

Creativity Meditations

Pebble on a beach
Autumn Leaves
Frosty Day
Cloud Gazing
Cosmic Journey

Pebble on a Beach

Notes

This meditation is to help children expand their imagination and think about the mineral world. Ask your child or children to find a stone or a pebble. Before you start, encourage the children to look at their stone and notice its texture, shape and colour. Children can show their stones to each other and compare them. When they are settled, ask the children to hold the stone in their hands and close their eyes.

Meditation

Close your eyes
Take a deep breath in through your nose
And breathe out slowly through your mouth
Return to normal breathing
in and out through your nose

It is a warm, windy day by the sea
See yourself walking along a beach
Seagulls are swooping down to the sea below
and calling out to eachother

The sun is shining on the water
and warming you
As you walk along the beach
notice the sound of the crunching of pebbles
under your feet

Pick up a small stone
Look at its colour, texture and shape
Feel the stone in your hand
It may be rough or smooth

Find a large flat rock to sit down on
and look towards the sea

See the waves rise and fall
Listen to the sounds of the sea giving you energy
and making you feel strong and alive

Smell the sea air
Feel the wind on your face
and blowing through your hair

When you next pick up a pebble
hold it in your hand
Think about where it comes from
and how its shape and texture may have changed
over the years

Take a deep breath in and breathe out
and when you are ready, open your eyes

Autumn Leaves

Notes

This exercise is intended for autumn time. It helps children to appreciate the change of seasons and use their imagination.

Collect a selection of autumn leaves of different colours, shapes and sizes and arrange them in the centre of the room or a place where they are clearly visible. Allow the children to pick them up and pass them around before they settle down for meditation.

Meditation

Close your eyes
Notice your breathing in and out
through your nose

See yourself walking in a park on a mild autumn day
Look down and notice a large red leaf
that has fallen in front of you
and pick it up

Look carefully at the colour of the leaf
Look at its size
The leaf may be as large as your hand
It may be smooth or rough

Now look up and see that the leaves of the trees
have many different colours
There may be yellow, gold, orange, red and brown leaves

The park has been transformed
from the green of summer
to the warm oranges and reds of autumn

There is a carpet of orange and brown leaves
that have fallen from the trees
to the ground underneath

In a few weeks it will be winter
and the branches of the trees may be bare

Then spring will arrive
with its green shoots, leaves and flowers
Followed by the bright colours of summer

The seasons are constantly changing
in the yearly cycle of life

Let's take more time to notice the changes
and enjoy each season as it greets us

Take a deep breath in together through your nose
Breathe out with a sigh
And open your eyes when you are ready

Frosty Day

Notes

This meditation encourages children to look at their environment and appreciate the beauty of a frosty day. This is a meditation to help children see and create a magical world using their senses and imagination. Share pictures of frosted trees, leaves and grass before starting the exercise.

Meditation

Close your eyes
Imagine it is a cold and frosty day
See yourself putting on a warm coat, hat, gloves and boots
When you are dressed open the door
And step outside and enter into an icy world

Take a deep breath in through your nose
As you breathe out
see misty breath coming from your mouth

Do this again.....breathe in the cool air
and breathe out the white misty air

See yourself walking across the frozen grass
There is the silence all around you
except for the crunch of the grass
underneath your boots

The grass, plants and trees that were once green
Are now covered with white frost

The sun appears from behind white clouds
and shines down on the glistening frost
Your icy world turns into shimmering whites and greys

See yourself picking up a leaf
Cold and wet to touch
Wipe off the frost to reveal
the green shiny texture beneath

Do this again with another object on the ground
It may be another leaf or a twig
or another item of your choice

See it covered with frost
And wipe it away to see what is underneath
Spend a few moments doing this

Continue to walk in the crunchy grass
and then pause
Breathe in the cool air through your nose
Breathe out the misty air through your mouth

Return back to this room
And open your eyes

Cloud Gazing

Notes

This practice stimulates the imagination. Take your child or children outside on a day when clouds are visible in a blue sky. Let the children sit or lie back on a mat and gaze at the clouds for at least five minutes. Allow them to call out the patterns or shapes they see in the clouds.

Ask the children to sit up again for the exercise. Explain to the children that they should keep their answers to any questions asked in the meditation in their heads until after the end of the exercise. Encourage the children to share their experiences after the meditation.

Meditation

Closing your eyes
Take a deep breath in through your nose
and breathe out slowly through your mouth

Think about the clouds you have been watching
Like balls of cotton wool floating up above
The many shades of white, yellow and grey
against a blue sky

Remember the colours, shapes and patterns
of the clouds
Did the shapes remind you
of a person, animal, bird, toy or anything else?

Think about the colours you noticed

Now see yourself sitting comfortably
on a fluffy cloud up in the sky
You feel light, as you float up higher
You feel peaceful and calm

Allow the cloud to transport you
over houses, fields, people and trees below
You can go wherever you wish

Journey further to a place in your imagination
you can visit mountains, forests, oceans or lakes
or go even further - into space
and visit a star or another planet

PAUSE for a few minutes

Take a deep breath in through your nose
And out through your mouth
And again in and out, ...in and out

With each breath find yourself carried back to this room
keeping in mind how you felt during the journey

Slowly return to this room
and when you are ready open your eyes

Cosmic Journey

Notes

This is an exercise to help to stimulate children's creative imagination and develop an appreciation of the solar system and beyond. Share a picture of the stars and planets including Earth to help evoke the sense of a cosmic adventure before commencing the exercise. Have drawing materials available for the children to use after the meditation.

Meditation

Close your eyes
And take a deep breath in through your nose
and breathe out through your mouth
Return to normal breathing
Gently breathing in and out through your nose

We are going on a special journey
into outer space
to see the solar system
of which our planet is a part

See yourself in a space ship
leaving planet Earth behind
to discover stars and planets far away

As you journey away from Earth
Look down and see our blue planet
moving further and further away

Then looking up, see a star or planet ahead in the distance
Travel towards the star or planet
and know that you are welcome to visit this place

Land your space ship
and see friendly beings coming to meet you

Look carefully at these beings
They may be taller or smaller than humans
Look at the colour of their skin
and notice if they have hair

The beings greet you and ask you about your home
In your mind, you can tell them about your planet
and where you live
what you do and how you spend your time

Let them take you around their planet
See many different creatures
Some may be similar to humans and animals on Earth
And some may be very different

Look and see if there are plants and trees
mountains and lakes
Notice the differences between this place and Planet Earth
Spend time looking around you and up at the sky above
It is now time to return to home
Find your space ship
and say goodbye to your new friends
Then travel back to planet Earth

PAUSE

Take a deep breath in through your nose
and breathe out through your mouth

Return to this room
and when you are ready open your eyes

Confidence Meditations

- The Sun (power)
- Secret Smile (self-confidence)
- Animal Adventure (courage)
- Your Loving Higher Self (protection)
- The Mountain (willpower)
- The Perfect Zone (competitions)

The Sun

Notes

The sun is energising and powerful and brings us light. This practice helps children to connect to their "inner sun" and will bring them confidence and energy. Before starting ask the children to place their hands over their heart centre in the centre of the chest so they are clear about its location.

It may also be helpful to share a photo of a field of wheat before you start.

Meditation

Gently close your eyes
Let's take three deep breaths together
Breathe in through your nose and breathe out
through your mouth
And again, breathe in and out, in and out

Return to normal breathing
in and out through your nose

See yourself walking into a field of wheat
on a warm summer's day
The sun is shining in a bright blue sky

Sit down amongst the wheat stalks
Feel the rays of light shining down on your body
The sun is giving you energy and strength

Take a deep breath in
Breathing in the sunlight into the top of your head
As you breathe out
let the light flow through your whole body

Do this again, breathing in the sunlight
and breathing out, let the golden rays reach
every part of you
Spreading the light through your whole body

Picture the sun in the centre of your chest
See it shining brightly
And let your sun shine right out of your body

This light is your own energy centre
Your own sun
Giving you energy and power

You can fill the whole room with your light
You can send your light out as far as you wish
Let it reach any person or place anywhere you wish

Keep sending out your light
whilst you breathe in and out
Continue for a few more breaths

When you are ready
slowly bring the energy back into your body
Take a deep breath in and breathe out slowly
Open your eyes when you are ready

Secret Smile

Notes

This practice is to help children feel loved and promotes self-confidence. It is based on the popular Buddhist secret smile meditation. Before you start the meditation smile at your child or children or ask the children to smile at the child sitting next to them. Let them see how a face "lights up" and experience the joy of a smile. Remind the children not to call out any answers during the meditation and that they can share their experiences afterwards.

Meditation

Close your eyes
Take a deep breath in through your nose
and breathe out through your mouth with a sigh

Keeping your eyes closed,
smile for a few seconds

PAUSE

Then rest your mouth

Think about how you felt inside when you smiled

PAUSE

Now think about something that makes you want to smile
It could be a person, an animal,
an object or a place that you love

Or it could be your own smiling face
or a time when you felt happy

Think about your smiling face
as you keep breathing in and out

And smile back at the picture in your mind
Send this smile to all parts inside your body
To your organs – your brain, heart, lungs, stomach
And to your skin, hair and bones
and the parts you do not often think of

Send the smile to every part of your body
Smile at your whole self
Now every cell in your body is smiling

See yourself sharing your smile
with your family, friends or pets
You can share the smile with anyone you wish

Keeping the smile on your face
Take a deep breath in and out through your nose
Open your eyes when you are ready

Animal Adventure

Notes

This is a confidence boosting exercise. Shamanic tradition believes that animal spirits reside in each individual adding to their power and bringing protection. Identifying the inner animal such as a tiger, bear or wolf allows the child to use their imagination and identify themselves with the qualities of that animal e.g. strength, courage and wisdom. A child may see an unexpected animal and there will be a good reason for the choice.

Ask the children not to call out during the meditation, but offer them the opportunity to share the name of their animal and its quality afterwards. You may also wish to provide drawing materials to let the children express what they saw during meditation.

Meditation

Close your eyes
Take a deep breath in through your nose
and breathe out through your mouth
Return to normal breathing
in and out through your nose

See yourself in a jungle
There are many interesting looking plants,
brightly coloured flowers,
and trees with dark green leaves

Hear the sounds of birds
high up in the branches of trees
Listen out for insects buzzing around
Smell the flowers and plants around you

See an animal appear before you
This animal is your friend
It is here to protect you
and help you feel strong

It can be any animal you wish
an elephant, lion, eagle, tiger, monkey or giraffe
or even a small animal or an insect

Take a good look at the animal you have chosen
Is it large or small?
Does it have fur or smooth skin?
How many legs does it have
Is there a tail?

Think about what you like about the animal you have chosen
Perhaps it is strong and brave
Wise and intelligent
Happy and playful

See yourself greeting the animal
and making friends with it

This is your special animal
It is always here for you
You can share any secrets with it
It can comfort you and be with you in anytime or any place

All you need to do is close your eyes
And call it back to you

Keep thinking about the animal
And take three deep breaths
In through your nose and out through your mouth
And again in and out.....in and out

Return back to the room
And slowly open your eyes

Your Loving Higher Self

Notes

This is a meditation for children who feel vulnerable. They may have been criticised or feel they have no friends and that they are alone or unloved. They are in need of love, comfort and protection. This exercise offers a tool to help that vulnerable child.

Meditation

Sitting comfortably with a straight back
Gently close your eyes

We are going to take three deep breaths together
Breathe in through your nose
and breathe out slowly through your mouth
And again, breathe in and breathe out slowly
One more time, breathing in and slowly breathing out

Return to normal breathing in and out through your nose
Think about how you are feeling right now

There may be times in our life
when we may feel hurt or unloved
Someone may say words that upset us
or we feel left out and alone

But remember this:
You are perfect exactly as you are
and there is nothing about you
that needs to change

In your mind, see a body of golden
white light surrounding you
a larger version of you
called your Higher Self

Allow this body of golden light
to wrap its arms around you
and fill you with love and light
comforting and protecting you

PAUSE

You can call on your Higher Self
to give you extra love and protection
at any time you feel you need it

Remember that you are never alone
You are always loved and protected

Let's take three more deep breaths together
Breathe in and breathe out,
And again, in and out….. in and out

When you ready, open your eyes

The Mountain

Notes

This meditation encourages children to fulfil their goals using willpower to reach the top of their 'mountain' whatever it may be. It builds confidence and also offers peace and steadiness.

Meditation

Close your eyes
In your mind see a large mountain
The mountain is covered with trees
and right at the top you can see white snow

Decide that you will climb the mountain
and reach the highest point – the summit

Take three deep breaths
Breathe in through your nose and out through your mouth
in and out……in and out

Starting at the bottom of the mountain
see yourself walking along a path
winding up the side of the mountain

The path becomes rocky ahead
Climb over the rocks
Taking care to keep your balance
keep walking straight on the path

Now take a rest for a few moments
Notice your breathing, steady and regular
and that the air is cooler as you go up the mountain
Enjoy the peace and quiet around you

The path becomes steeper
Start climbing up using your arms and legs
Stretch your arms and pull yourself up
using your legs to keep you strong and balanced
Keep going up and up

Taking another rest
notice the cool air as you breathe in and out
Look down at the view below
See how small the trees are

The top of the mountain is ahead
A bit more effort and you will be there
Take the last few steps
and you have reached the top!

Think about how you feel to reach your goal

PAUSE

Take three deep breaths
Breathing in through your nose
and out through your mouth with a sigh
And again in and out…in and out

Return to the room
and open your eyes when you are ready

The Perfect Zone

Notes

It is common to have the "butterflies in the tummy" sensation before competitions or matches. The question is how to transform that feeling so it enhances performance. This practice may assist by taking the child back to a time and place when they performed well and encourage them to recall the words and feelings they experienced at the time. A suggested affirmation is included and there is an opportunity for children to create their own affirmation.

Remind the children to keep the answers to the questions in the meditation in their heads and let them share their experiences afterwards if they wish.

Meditation

Close your eyes
Take a deep breath in through your nose
and breathe out slowly through your mouth

Think about a time
when you gave your best performance
or played your best game
This is called your Perfect Zone

Think about you how you feel inside
How did you look?
What words were you saying to yourself?
What were you doing?

Now in this very moment
see yourself feeling and looking exactly as you did
in the Perfect Zone

See yourself doing the same actions
thinking the same thoughts
and saying the same words to yourself before you start

In your mind go through the performance or the game
See yourself doing every single movement slowly
Take your time and perform each move as
perfectly as possible

You are now in the Perfect Zone
You are filled with confidence and with positive energy

In your head, say to yourself:
"I am confident, I am filled positive energy"

You can think of any other words
that you know will help you
In your head, say the words to yourself now
And repeat them

Remember the special words
and the positive thoughts and feelings
and use them whenever you need them
in any place and at any time

Take a deep breath in through your nose
and breathe out through your mouth
When you are ready open your eyes

Self Healing Meditations

The Candle
Magical Waters
Shower of Light
The Rainbow
Healing Heart

The Candle

Notes

This is a healing meditation that allows children to think about themselves as a body of light and shows them how to direct and grow their light. Place a lighted candle in the centre of the room. Seat the children in a circle around the candle so it is visible to all of them. If possible, lower the lights once the children are settled.

Meditation

Keeping your eyes open, look at the candle flame
Notice the colours of the flame,
You may see white, blue, yellow, orange, red
See the light coming out from the flame

Close your eyes,
keeping a picture of the candle in your mind
Take three deep breaths
breathing in through your nose and out through your mouth
Breathe in and out ……. and in and out

As you return to normal gentle breathing
through your nose
in your mind see a picture of the candle and the flame

Now see a tiny flame in the middle of your forehead
Let the flame become brighter and larger
until the light fills your head
and then fills your whole body

See yourself as body of light
In your head, say to yourself
"I am a Being of Light"

Now let the light flow out of your body
Let it fill the space around you
Until the light fills the whole room

You can spread the light even further
outside the room and beyond
Send it out as far as you wish

Take three more deep breaths,
In through your nose and out through your mouth
again in and out….in and out

Allow the flame to become smaller and smaller
and return to its original size inside your head

Take one more breath in and breathe out
Slowly open your eyes
And return to look at the candle

Magical Waters

Notes

This is a meditation that helps us to appreciate the healing qualities of water. Positive thoughts and emotions enhance the quality of the water. Dr Masaru Emoto, author of 'The Hidden Messages from Water', carried out research on water for many years and published photographs of water crystals showing how they are affected by various positive and negative thoughts and emotions. He has produced a number of books including a picture book for children that I highly recommend for children.[11]

Play gentle classical music in the background and leave it on quietly during the meditation to create a peaceful atmosphere.

Meditation

Gently close your eyes
Let's take a breath in together through the nose
And breathe out gently through your mouth

Return to normal breathing
in and out through your nose

See yourself by the side of a lake
It is a magical lake
The water is clear and blue

Walk closer to the water's edge
Take a step into the cool water
and another
until both feet are in the water

The water in the lake is special
It has healing powers
that allow you feel healthy and happy

As you walk a bit further into the lake
let go of any thoughts or feelings
that may upset you

Take one step at a time
Until your whole body is covered
With the healing water

The waters wash away
any pains in your body
or sad feelings or thoughts

If you wish you can start to swim
As you swim, breathe in the magic from the water
As you breathe out,
let the magical water flow through you

Turn and float on your back
Experience the peace and calm
And the magic of stillness inside you

Swim or walk back to edge of lake
Step out of the water
feeling refreshed and healthy

Sit down by the edge of the lake
The sun is shining down
warming you until you are dry

Take three deep breaths slowly in through your nose
and out through your mouth
In and out....in and out

Open your eyes when you are ready
and notice how you feel now

Shower of Light

Notes

This is a powerful and effective healing exercise to help cleanse and energise the whole body. The light can be directed to any part of the body that is injured or hurt either physically or emotionally. The visualisation of an egg or shield around the body has been described as offering protection from environmental pollution, electronic devices and radiation.

Meditation

Gently close your eyes
Sitting upright with a straight spine

We are going to take a deep breath in together
through the nose
and breathe out through our mouth with a sigh

See a shower of golden white light
from above the top of your head
flowing down over your body
covering your front and back all the way down to your feet

Take a deep breath in through your nose
and breathe in the golden white light
As you breathe out through your nose
spread the light to every cell of your body

Repeat this again, breath in the light
and as you breathe out
spread the light through your body

You can direct the healing light
to any part of your body
that needs healing or comfort

Send the light rays wherever you wish
and continue to breathe

PAUSE

Each time you have a shower or wash your hands
you can close your eyes and in your mind
see the water as golden white light
healing and making you feel better

Now see the light surrounding you
forming an egg shape around your whole body
This egg of light will protect you
at anytime and in any place

PAUSE

Take a deep breath in through your nose
and breathe out through your mouth
Open your eyes when you are ready

The Rainbow

Notes

This exercise helps with self-healing using the colours of the rainbow. The colours represent light frequencies that combined together form white light, a healing and protective light. Each colour has a different frequency from red, orange, yellow, green, blue, indigo to violet. Before starting the meditation, show the children a picture of a rainbow and point out the colours, particularly indigo, which is a less well known colour.

Distribute paper and pencils or paint to the children to use to draw or paint pictures of rainbows after the exercise.

Meditation

Close your eyes
Take a deep breath in through your nose
and breathe out slowly through your mouth
Return to normal breathing
in and out through your nose

In your mind, picture a rainbow
See the colours of the rainbow
red, orange, yellow
green, blue, indigo and violet

Imagine that you are sitting in the rainbow
We are going to find how each colour makes you feel

Think about the red colour – like blood making your body strong
Then move to orange – making you feel warm and happy
Then yellow – like the sun, shining brightly and giving you confidence
Now green – like the trees and plants, bringing love and joy
Blue – like the waves in the sea,
making you want to swim, dance, sing or draw
Indigo – deep, darkest blue giving you magical powers to see and hear deep inside yourself
Violet – like violet flowers, helping you to find peace, quiet and stillness inside

Pick one of the colours
Take a deep breath in

and let the coloured light spread through your whole body
As you breathe out, let the light heal any aches or pains
or any sad thoughts or feelings in your body

You can now choose another colour or keep the same one
Taking a deep breath in,
let that coloured light fill your whole body
and as your breathe out
send it to any part that needs healing
Remember that you can fill yourself with coloured light
anytime you wish
If you feel unhappy or hurt in your mind or body
you can come back to this place and heal yourself

If you need more love then see a pink colour
in the centre of your heart
and let the pink colour fill your whole body

When all the colours of the rainblow are mixed together,
white light is created
a special light that can protect you and heal you
Take a deep breath and see a white light
all around and inside your body
filling every space

You are safe in this white light,
Stay here a bit longer

PAUSE

Then let's take a deep breath in and out together
And come back to this room and open your eyes.

Healing Heart

Notes

There are seven centres or "chakras", wheels of energy located up the back of the spine, from the base of the spine, to the sacral, solar plexus, heart, throat, third eye up to top of the head. This practice identifies two of the centres, heart and solar plexus and can be used to transform emotions such as anger or anxiety to peace and love.

Before you start this exercise, show the children a picture of 'The Seven Chakras' in Resources and point out the solar plexus and heart centre. Let the children place their hands on each of these areas of their own body before you begin. For more detailed information please refer to the Resources and References section.

Meditation

Close your eyes
Take a deep breath in through your nose
and breathe out slowly through your mouth
And again, take a deep breath in and breathe out slowly

Bring your hands up above your belly button
to your stomach area
This is the place where you may sometimes
feel tight or uncomfortable
Notice how you feel right now

Take a deep breath in
and breathe out slowly out through your mouth

Take your hands away
and let them rest gently by your sides
Continue to breathe gently in and out through your nose

Now bring your attention to your heart centre
and in your mind
see a golden white light right in the middle
As you slowly breathe in and out
the light becomes brighter and brighter

Now with invisible hands
see yourself gently lifting up
any tightness or pain
from your stomach area up to your heart centre

In this place, let any tension, pain or unhappy feelings
be transformed into positive feelings
of love and peace

Take a deep breath in and breathe out slowly
Spend a few more moments here
And notice how you feel now

PAUSE

Return to normal breathing
Listen to the sound of your breath
When you are ready open your eyes

Resources and References

The Seven Chakras

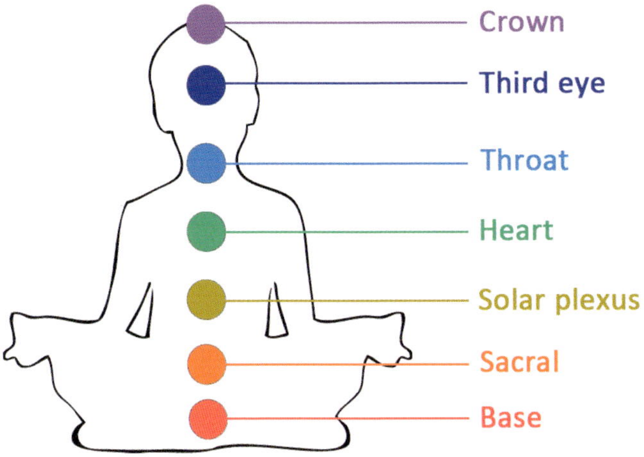

For more information see
Subtle Body: Essence and Shadow by David V. Tansley.

Music for Meditation

Millenia perform Tranquillity

Tranquility II by David Sun

The Sound of Birdsong by Nigel Tucker

Ultimate OM by Jonathan Goldman

https://www.youtube.com/watch?v=CYXG9rG0Jf0
(Ocean waves)

https://www.youtube.com/watch?v=QX4j_zHAlw8
(Calming sea)

https://www.youtube.com/watch?v=NK2_bcQcoD4
(Birdsong)

Sprays

10 drops each of two or more essential oils (see below)
100 ml purified or filtered water

Add essential oil drops to purified water
in a small spray bottle, for example:
Calming – lavender, ylang ylang, chamomile, sandalwood
Uplifting – orange, lemongrass, grapefruit, peppermint, rose
Cleansing – frankincense, lemon, tea tree

Take care to spray at least one foot above the
heads of the children.

References

1. http://www.intothewoodsnursery.co.uk/benefits-of-outdoor-play.html
2. Alice Bailey, Education in the New Age, p 13-14
3. www.steinerwaldorf.org/steiner-education/what-is-steiner-education/
4. Dr Norma J. Milanovich and Dr Shirley D. McCune, The Light Shall Set You Free, p 279
5. Alice Bailey, From Intellect to Intuition, p 99
6. ibid p109
7. Michal J Eastcott, The Silent Path, p 62
8. ibid pp 62-63
9. ibid p 63
10. The Harvard Gazette, When Mind meets Science, by Alvin Powell, April 2018 https://news.harvard.edu/gazette/story/2018/04/harvard-researchers-study-how-mindfulness-may-change-the-brain-in-depressed-patients/
11. www.emotopeaceproject.net

Thank you to Lucis Press, the Sundial House Group for Creative Meditation* and Dr Norma Milanovich for permission to use the quotations.

*A correspondence Training Course in Creative Meditation for parents and adults in available from the Centre for Creative Meditation see www.creativemeditation.net.

Further Reading

Spinning Inward by Maureen Murdock

What our Children Teach Us by Piero Ferrucci

The Invisible Classroom by Kirke Olson

The Power of Now by Eckhart Tolle

Subtle Body by David V. Tansley

The Miracle of Mindfulness by Thich Nhat Hanh

The Hidden Messages in Water by Masaru Emoto

Final Words

It has been a joy to write this book. I would like to thank my beautiful children, Alexander, Mia and Chiara for inspiring me to teach children's yoga and meditation and my husband Laurence for his humour and keeping me grounded. Thank you also to my parents, Helen and Eric, and sisters Nicole and Simone for their love and support.

I am grateful to my teacher, Gillian Roslin Wright, who has been a constant source of inspiration and wisdom over the past few decades. A huge thank you goes to Dr Debra Kalmanowitz for her encouragement and advice and to Shirley Henen for her wonderful guidance. Thanks also to Lisa Goodkind for her practical and wise advice and to Allison Pearlman for her support throughout this journey.

My dream is for parents, children and their families to practice meditation together on a regular basis and for teachers in mainstream educational centres to increasingly incorporate daily meditation into their curriculum together with more creative arts and outdoor activities in nature.

Please join me in making this dream a reality.

Testimonials

Shirley Henen
Author, Healer, Teacher

"In a changing world, the heightened energies and anxieties bring tensions and difficulties to all. Our children need to be equipped to deal with what surrounds them. This beautiful book brings guidance to parents and teachers - a tool to facilitate awareness of downtime that opens a pathway to connection, inner peace, release, strength and love."

Hamish Hendry
Founder of Astanga Yoga London, Yoga instructor

"Michelle's book is a delight to read for adults and kids alike. Michelle has brought together old traditional teachings and modern thought. There is enough to keep you interested and it's simple enough not to bog you down. So it's really relevant for today's children who find it difficult to switch off. The practices Michelle passes on help open the heart so that connection to the world becomes easier. Meditate, smile, repeat."

Rochelle Hope
Primary School Teacher and Children's Yoga teacher

"Parents liked the special, quiet time with their children and felt that the children were very relaxed afterwards. They also described a feeling of peacefulness in the house afterwards and also an air of anticipation beforehand. All parents felt the meditations were an exciting prospect for the future and thought that both parents and children would benefit hugely if they could be incorporated into their lives. All parents agreed that children's mental health is a massive issue and this is a great step towards what is necessary to help children in the future."

Allison Pearlman
Yoga Teacher & Owner Yoga Zone

"This beautifully written book will be a very helpful guide for me when teaching my children's yoga classes. It's very easy to follow and implement - I particularly like the different categories. Children will definitely benefit from these magic meditations as I'm sure the parents and teachers will too!"